A BIBLICAL STUDY

YOUR LIFE'S COURSE AND YOUR LIFE'S CALL

BASED ON 2 TIMOTHY 1:8-11 AND 2 TIMOTHY 4:7

Dr. Ronald E. Cottle

Your Life's Course and Your Life's Call

REC Ministries
664 Sweetwater Drive
Cataula, GA 31804
www.roncottle.com

TABLE OF CONTENTS

A WORD FROM THE EDITOR

With great joy, Dr. Cottle and I present this small book to you. It may be small in size, but it is big in truth and importance to every leader in the Kingdom of God.

In its pages, you will discover how you can continue to live on in this world after you enter eternity. One truly can live forever!

It is my honor to edit and publish these works. May you treasure the words of this book as I do.

Dr. Thomas Hale
Editor and Multiplier of Ron Cottle Ministries

INTRODUCTION

The Apostle Paul, before he was the Apostle Paul, was a notorious persecutor of the early Church. We first encounter him in Acts 8:1, when Paul, then called Saul, was approving the execution of Stephen before going to terrorize the Church in Syria. Later, after he was converted and was pouring his very life out for the establishment of the Church he once persecuted, he said this about his former life:

> 3 For we are the circumcision, who worship God in the Spirit, rejoice in Christ Jesus, and have no confidence in the flesh, 4 though I also might have confidence in the flesh. If anyone else thinks he may have confidence

in the flesh, I more so: 5 circumcised the eighth day, of the stock of Israel, of the tribe of Benjamin, a Hebrew of the Hebrews; concerning the law, a Pharisee; 6 concerning zeal, persecuting the church; concerning the righteousness which is in the law, blameless (Philippians 3:3-6).

He describes how he had once tamed his flesh for Judaism. He describes his life as a devout and zealous "Hebrew of Hebrews." When he says that "concerning the Law," he was "a Pharisee," he conveys the seriousness with which he approached his faith. He even claims that, according to the law, he was "blameless."

Paul had the unique experience and temperament to be the one God would conscript to work out and preach the great and mighty doctrines of justification by faith alone.

Paul was the perfect person to preach the gospel of freedom and to show the futility of legalism.

This book is about the way God has built, not only Paul, but all of His children, with certain inclinations, gifts, talents, and life experiences. Examining these will allow the disciple of Jesus to begin to discern the course and call that God has on his life. This is the task of every faithful follower of Jesus Christ.

CHAPTER 1 – COURSE MEANS JOURNEY

"I have finished the course."

Course means "journey" (*dromon* - race, career, itinerary). Paul's course was based on an itinerary marked out in advance. God assigns a definite course for everyone. It is marked and calculated in advance.

2 Timothy 1:8-11

> 8 Therefore do not be ashamed of the testimony of our Lord, nor of me His prisoner, but share with me in the sufferings for the gospel according to the power of God, 9 who has saved us and called us with a holy

(set apart, unique) calling, not according to our works, but according to His own purpose and grace which was given to us in Christ Jesus before time began, 10 but has now been revealed by the appearing of our Savior (not the second coming of King Jesus, but our conversion is mentioned here) Jesus Christ, who has abolished death and brought life and immortality to light (in us) through the gospel, 11 to which I was appointed a preacher, an apostle, and a teacher of the Gentiles.

This includes both Paul's career direction and its distance. Paul rejoiced at the end that he "fought the good fight...finished the race...kept the faith" (2 Timothy 4:7).

· Fought the good fight (*agōn* – agony)

· Finished the course (*dromon* – race)

· Kept the faith (*pistis* – reliance on Christ)

Watchman Nee says: "I believe God placed this course or itinerary before Paul on the day he believed in the Lord."

Galatians 1:15-16

> 15 But when it pleased God, who separated me from my mother's womb and called me through His grace, 16 to reveal His Son in (not to but inside) me, that I might preach Him among the Gentiles, I did not immediately confer with flesh and blood.

YOUR LIFE'S COURSE AND YOUR LIFE'S CALL

He set me apart from my mother's womb and called
me through His grace (favour).

– Watchman Nee

While he was in his mother's womb, God set him
apart – his course was designed and assigned.

– Watchman Nee

Set Out on Your Course

When Paul was saved, he set out on this course (journey, career, race). This shows that our preparation and initiation (calling, anointing) as a man or woman of God and minister of His kingdom are determined by God when we are still in our mother's womb.

Look again at **2 Timothy 1:8-11, adding verse 12**:

8 Therefore do not be ashamed of the testimony of our Lord, nor of me His prisoner, but share with me in the sufferings for the gospel according to the power of God, 9 who has saved us and called us with a holy calling, not according to our works, but according to His own purpose and grace which was given to us in Christ Jesus before time began, 10 but has now been revealed by

the appearing of our Savior Jesus Christ, who has abolished death and brought life and immortality to light through the gospel, 11 to which I was appointed a preacher, an apostle, and a teacher of the Gentiles. 12 For this reason I also suffer these things; nevertheless, I am not ashamed, for I know whom I have believed and am persuaded that He is able to keep what I have committed to Him until that Day.

Paul says in 1 Corinthians 9:16, "For if I preach the gospel, I have nothing to boast of, for necessity is laid upon me; yes, woe is me if I do not preach the gospel!" God had revealed the course for Paul, the race, and "woe is" Paul if he did not run it.

God Reveals the Path

This is one of the deep mysteries of the faith. We live our lives in what God has created as real time. God knows all, and we at the start know nothing until He reveals it to us. We did not know Him until He apprehended us. We don't know ourselves until He shows us to us, and we certainly do not know what we are to do until we have been shown the path ahead of us, and sometimes not until we have walked it.

In Ephesians 2:10 Paul says, "For we are His workmanship, created in Christ Jesus for good works, which God prepared beforehand that we should walk in them."

Created in His Image

We are His workmanship (*poiēma* - product, a thing made), created (*ktisthentes* - shaped, formed) in Christ

Jesus for good works (*ergois* - toil). God thought us up and made us who we are. He formed us. He crafted us like a Master Craftsman for a purpose, a "good" *toil.* And what is this toil? It is something which was prepared in advance (*proētoimasen* - predestined) for us that we should walk it out (*peripatēsōmen)* as our way of life. He has called us to a toil, work, that is to be our *way of life.* This has profound implications for the concept of work.

In the beginning, God created man in His very image. **Genesis 1:26-28:**

> 26 Then God said, "Let Us make man in Our image, according to Our likeness; let them have dominion over the fish of the sea, over the birds of the air, and over the cattle, over all the earth and over every creeping thing that creeps on the earth." 27 So God created

man in His own image; in the image of God He created him; male and female He created them. 28 Then God blessed them, and God said to them, "Be fruitful and multiply; fill the earth and subdue it; have dominion over the fish of the sea, over the birds of the air, and over every living thing that moves on the earth."

We Were Made for Specific Work

We see from these verses the cultural mandate to be fruitful and go about subduing the earth. We are to work. In Genesis 2 it says that God placed the man in the garden to work it (Genesis 2:15). These verses tell us that God has made us and called us to work. The verses above from Ephesians 2 and 2 Timothy show us that God has made us for *specific work.* What work is that? The work that He has "prepared in advance." God has made each of us for a specific purpose. We should say with Paul, "woe is me if I do not…" The blank is filled in by God Himself.

In the next chapter we will explore the idea that the clues to our vocational calling and course are found in us even *before* we are saved.

CHAPTER 2 – BEFORE WE WERE SAVED

Every experience we had before we were saved was under God's sovereign arrangement. Look at Paul. Before Jesus saved him on the road to Damascus, God had already put key characteristics into him and put him through important experiences. He was a serious student of the Torah. When God put the Holy Spirit into him, all that information was activated toward Christ.

He was zealous for the name of the Lord, though he was wrong in his ignorance. His passion was redirected when the Lord called him. God took that same passion and intensified it, sending him far and wide into the jaws of the lion.

God Prepares You for Your Calling

If you know any effective ministers today, you can ask them about their lives, and they will tell you a story of the ways God was preparing them for what He would call them to do later in life. One man was given a mind for organization and leadership. Before he was a Christian, he was the manager of a marina. The lessons he learned about making the business more profitable, were put to use in building a network of effective churches. His accounting background was put to use in the accounting of the churches. His PhD in speech communication was taken over by a call to preach the Word.

Another man was put through great turmoil in his life. Insecurities dominated his childhood, and in adolescence he struggled to make it with people. He developed a powerful sense of what others were thinking, so that he could please them and gain their approval. Then Jesus apprehended him. He redeemed those qualities first born out of a sinful fear of man. Because of his own emotional pain, now healed and removed, he had a deep understanding of the pain of others and human nature in general. Because he had developed tremendous people skills, he was able to genuinely connect with almost anyone easily. Because he had cultivated a keen sense of humor, he had become extremely winsome. All of which God appropriated for His own purposes.

In yet one more example, I knew a man who was the general manager of a Walmart Superstore. These gargantuan stores are made up of a massive number of moving parts and systems, and they also employ hordes of workers. When the corporation offered to promote him to a regional manager position, that is, one who oversees several Walmart stores, he took up a call to ministry and pastoring. He left the corporate world of retail and put his gifts to use in the Church. After completing a seminary degree, he was hired by a fairly large church, which under his leadership and skill, became an enormous congregation made up of several locations. God had promoted him to regional manager of His Church! He then gave the man a vision to resource and staff small rural churches all over his state. This is a good illustration of what we are saying. God puts the skills and gifts in the man or woman *before* He calls him or her. It is God who prepares all these things.

God gives us our distinctive characters, our temperaments, our inclinations, and our virtues.

– Watchman Nee

No one goes through any experience by accident.

– Watchman Nee

Every Experience is Part of God's Sovereign Arrangement

No person inherits a character trait by accident; everything is under God's sovereign hand.

– Watchman Nee

God made provisions long ago for our natural abilities and experiences. He has prepared us for our life's commission from our mother's womb. Paul's course was set long before his conversion, as was ours, yours, and mine.

Consider the blessing to one who is suffering who meets another who has suffered the same things and can minister to them from a place of experience and wisdom. God uses everything for His purposes.

Let us look one more time at our verses in 2 Timothy 1 and break them down further.

2 Timothy 1:8

8 Therefore do not be ashamed of the testimony of our Lord, nor of me His prisoner, but share with me in the sufferings for the gospel according to the power of God.

- Testimony is *marturion* – *martus* – witness, judicial witness (legal), sworn in.
- Prisoner is *desmios* – bound together, joined by ligaments, chained together as to a guard.

Paul is encouraging Timothy to keep going and to "fan into flame" the gift he was given when Paul laid his hands on him and commissioned him (2 Timothy 1:6). Paul does not want Timothy or anyone else to be ashamed of him because of his suffering. On the contrary, it is Paul's suffering that is making him more effective for ministry.

Paul knows that he is suffering according to the plan and grace of God.

2 Timothy 1:9

> 9 who has saved us and called us with a holy calling, not according to our works, but according to His own purpose and grace which was given to us in Christ Jesus before time began,

- Called, is *kalleō, and* Calling is *klesis* - an invitation, urging, summons.
- Purpose is *protithemi* – *prothesis* – course, itinerary
- Grace is *charis* – grace, favor.

God Calls Everyone to His Purpose

Paul explains that God has "saved us and called us." Notice two things. First, Paul does not say that God has saved "me" and called "me," that is, Paul only. In Paul's mind, this is how God calls and treats everyone. Everyone who is converted to Christ is not only *saved*, but also *called*. And that is the second thing: salvation comes with calling and purpose. This purpose was given along with His grace in Christ before time began. This is astounding. Our course was set before time began. Our itinerary was laid out before us to walk in, by the grace of our all-knowing God.

2 Timothy 1:10

> 10 but has now been revealed by the appearing of our Savior Jesus Christ, who has abolished death and brought life and immortality to light through the gospel,

- Revealed is *phaneroō* – manifest, render apparent, existential.

- Appearing is *epiphaneia* – the epiphany of our purpose now available due to our conversion.

- Light is *photizō* – to shine upon this purpose in order to make us see.

Salvation Was Destined for Us

This salvation was destined for us since the foundation of the world, and so were our calling and course. When Christ came into Paul's life, suddenly everything about his life made sense. When He comes into the life of every believer it is that way. So much of the trial and training of our early, unconverted life begins to make sense. This is especially true when one has suffered hardship. Christ comes in, and in His light, the hardship brings great wisdom to help us to better understand ourselves and to assist others who are suffering in the same ways.

Your Purpose Established Before Time Began

When something is revealed, it is made *manifest.* It appears. It is an abstraction that is made into a concrete reality. Paul says that the "purpose and grace was given to us before time began." Your calling is a reality. It was a reality when you were born because it was a reality long *before* you were born. You might say *it is written on the wind.* Imagine that! Your God knew you intimately long before He went about creating you. When He did create you, it was because He had a purpose for you to serve Him and glorify His name by your life and work. How amazing!

Then, just at the right time, He manifested His grace for you in Christ Jesus. Which caused a manifestation of your purpose! Paul goes on in 2 Timothy 1:11, turning it intimately personal and inward in his own life:

11 to which I was appointed a preacher, an apostle, and a teacher of the Gentiles.

- Appointed is *tithemi* – set, established.
- Preacher is *kerux* – proclaimer, announcer.
- Teacher is *didaskalos* -- explainer, clarifier, applicator.
- Gentiles is *ethnoi* -- nations, Paul was an apostle (sent one) to the uncircumcision, the gentiles, the nations.

Find Your Calling

Paul was "established" as a "proclaimer." What has God established you to do and to be in His kingdom? Look to your past. Look at the things you have found yourself good at. Look especially at your mistakes, your failures, and your pain. The clues are there. God will reveal in time.

He will impress Himself upon your interests and desires if you will spend time in His presence.

CONCLUSION/APPLICATION

Imagine what would happen if all of God's people were willing to take up the course and calling of their life and walk the path that God has for them. Could we evangelize the world? Could we eradicate much of the suffering in this world, as God manifests His grace through the generosity and gifts of His people? Surely there will be some suffering until the return of Christ, but just as Christ used His ministry to help the sick, poor, and oppressed as a sign of His already come and coming kingdom, God can use His Church to do the same.

God is the "World's Greatest Economist." He wastes nothing. He has chaperoned and choreographed *your life up to now*. All you need to do is align yourself with His purpose (course, call), and you will release His grace in you. He will show it to you and make it plain. Say with Paul, "Woe is me if I don't..." Learn to be driven by God's purpose for you. You may be stumbling down the road, inch by inch, looking for the path, but you will see it, and He will bless you in it.

Come, Holy Spirit, and redeem our gifts and experiences. Conscript us for Your service and use what You have given us to do Your will, to gain glory for Yourself, and to bring about the Great Day when Jesus returns and establishes His kingdom on the earth. Amen

ABOUT THE AUTHOR

Dr. Ronald E. Cottle has been serving the body of Christ for more than six decades. He has extensive experience in teaching, pastoring, public speaking, education administration and both radio and television.

He has developed more than one hundred advanced courses of Christian development and biblical training and has authored more than one hundred books encompassing ministry, leadership, biblical studies, and church development.

Dr. Cottle's teaching style has been called "scholarship on fire" by those who have attended his lectures. His unique style always contains the compassion of a shepherd, the urgency of a prophet and the wisdom of a statesman.

His thoughts and counsel are straightforward, dynamic, and powerful. His teachings will help today's spiritual leaders and other sincere "thinking Christians" to discover the mystery and the majesty of the Bible.

Dr. Cottle has earned a Bachelor of Arts (A.B.) degree from Florida Southern College, Lakeland, Florida; a Master of Divinity (M.Div.) from Lutheran Theological Seminary, Columbia, South Carolina; and a Doctor of Philosophy (Ph.D.) in Religion from the University of Southern California, Los Angeles. He also earned a Master of Science in Education (M.S.Ed.) and a Doctor of Education (Ed.D.) from U.S.C.

FOR MORE INFORMATION ABOUT DR. RON COTTLE AND HIS NUMEROUS BOOKS AND TEACHINGS, GOTO: www.roncottle.com.

THE COTTLE LIBRARY

Dr. Cottle has worked tirelessly in his home office for the past two decades compiling his five hundred notebooks, fifty plus college courses, fifty plus books, hundreds of sermon outlines, publications, articles, and newsletters. Dr. Cottle and Dr. Thomas Hale are cataloging everything into an online library.

The library contains digital files (PDF and Microsoft Word) available for download, streaming audio files and streaming video files.

Please visit the library at: www.cottlelibrary.com.

www.ingramcontent.com/pod-product-compliance
Lightning Source LLC
Chambersburg PA
CBHW061647130726
47996CB00003B/1500